Gray Whales
on the Go

By Renée Carver

Scott Foresman
is an imprint of

Glenview, Illinois • Boston, Massachusetts • Chandler, Arizona •
Upper Saddle River, New Jersey

Photographs

Every effort has been made to secure permission and provide appropriate credit for photographic material. The publisher deeply regrets any omission and pledges to correct errors called to its attention in subsequent editions.

Unless otherwise acknowledged, all photographs are the property of Pearson Education, Inc.

Photo locators denoted as follows: Top (T), Center (C), Bottom (B), Left (L), Right (R), Background (Bkgd)

ISBN 13: 978-0-328-46910-9
ISBN 10:   0-328-46910-6

3 4 5 6 7 8 9 10 V010 13 12 11 10

Summer

This gray whale is in the Arctic Ocean. The Arctic is a cold place. But in summer, the water is a little warmer.

In summer, whales can find food in the Arctic. This whale must eat lots of food now. She won't eat again for many months.

Fall

Now it's late fall. The water is colder. It's time for the whales to migrate. That means they swim from one place to another place.

Winter

Now it's winter. The whales left the cold waters of the Arctic about 55 days ago. They migrated south.

They swam 24 hours a day. The waters here are much warmer. Mother whales will have their babies here.

People come to the warm waters too. They come to watch the whales. They take pictures of them. They want to see a mother whale and her calf.

The whales stay here all winter. Biologists study them. They listen to the whales' hearts. They watch them play. They watch how a mother whale takes care of her calf.

Spring

Now it's spring. Something tells the whales that it's time to migrate again. They will go back to the Arctic. They can find lots of food in the cooler waters there.

Biologists count how many mother and baby whales swim by. See you next year, whales!

The whales are back in the Arctic Ocean. They migrated about 5,500 miles. Each mother whale used up about 8 tons of whale blubber!

They are ready to eat . . . and eat . . . and eat.